WE THE PEOPLE

The First Americans

When ice blankets you call glaciers
were moving, slowly moving,
we found an open passage
between their frozen walls.
And we took that rich green passage,
in small bands we took that passage,
following the bison,
        following the game,
                finding as we followed
                        nuts and berries,
                                elk and deer.

Mother Earth and Father Sun,
hear the voices of your children,
thankful voices of your children:
for the gifts you made appear!

Ours were the first voices.
The first voices were The People.
Now we whisper
when the winds blow.
Remember we were here.

TERRA   INCOGNITA

WE
THE
PEOPLE

poems by **Bobbi Katz**

illustrations by *Nina Crews*

GREENWILLOW BOOKS
An Imprint of HarperCollinsPublishers

For Virginia

Photographic collages were made from a combination of archival images and photographed material. The final collages were completed electronically in Photoshop.
See pages 101–102 for additional information and photo credits.

The following poems were first published in *American History Poems* by Bobbi Katz (New York: Scholastic Professional Books, 1998): "The First Americans," "A Pilgrim Boy," "My Favorite Time," "A Tea Merchant's Daughter," "A Conversation on the Edge of War," "The Challenge," "Inauguration Day Thoughts," "My White House Education," "A Seaman's Chantey," "Wondering," "Career Plans," "Freedom!," "At the Station," "A Bird's-Eye View of the Civil War," "A Letter to China," "A Pioneer Woman Looks Back," "A Useless Gadget," "Will We Be a New State?," "A Matter of Life or . . . Death," "A Gold Miner's Tale," "America!," "A Song for Suffrage," "The Assembly Line," "A New Deal," "On the Way to Californ-I-A!," "Shopping," "On the Home Front," "The Moondust Footprint." Reprinted by permission of the author.

Library of Congress Cataloging-in-Publication Data
Katz, Bobbi.
  We the people / by Bobbi Katz ; with illustrations by Nina Crews.
    p.   cm.
    "Greenwillow Books."
    Summary: A collection of sixty-five original poems that depict people and events throughout the history of the United States.   ISBN 0-688-16531-1 (trade). ISBN 0-688-16532-X (lib. bdg.)
    1. United States—History—Juvenile poetry. 2. United States—Biography—Juvenile poetry. 3. Children's poetry, American. [1. United States—History—Poetry. 2. American poetry.]
  I. Crews, Nina, ill.   II. Title.   PS3561.A7518 W4 2000   811'.54—dc21   99-050009

1 2 3 4 5 6 7 8 9 10   First Edition

A NOTE ABOUT READING THE POEMS:
The poems in this book are ideal for reading aloud or performing. Some of the poems can be read by an ensemble, such as "Speaking Up at the Miner's Meeting" on page 73 and "What Do You Think of President Eisenhower?" on page 74. The poems on pages 6, 15, 42, 52, and 62 are poems for two voices. They can be read aloud in much the same way that musicians play a duet: One person reads the left-side part; the other person reads the right-side part; both read together when the same words are on the same horizontal line.

CONTENTS

At the Edge of the 19th Century

At the Edge of the 20th Century

❖ At the Edge of the 21st Century

Arriving in Virginia

NATHANIEL PEACOCK
near the James River, Virginia, April 26, 1607

The swell of the waves
became part of me.
Five months on the *Godspeed*.
Five months at sea.
My feet don't seem to understand.
They're not on a deck.
They're on land! They're on land!
And all about us green, green, green!
The tallest trees I've ever seen.
Oh, lucky, lucky, lucky me!
This green land is my destiny.
A hundred men
and boys—just four—
with a feast of green
to explore . . . to explore!

1585 Sir Walter Raleigh sends
settlers to Roanoke Island,
North Carolina.

1607 The Virginia Company
starts a permanent English
colony in Jamestown.

1

A Message for the Settlers

CHIEF WAHUNSONACOCK (POWHATAN)
Jamestown, Virginia, 1615

You were few and we were many.
You were weak and we were strong.
You were hungry and we brought you corn.
Did not my own daughter, Pocahontas, bring you corn?
Why should you seek to destroy us,
we who have brought you food?
Oh, Coat-wearing People,
did we not save you from death?
Have you forgotten the crown of copper
sent to me by your King?

> Is it not better to trade in peace?
> Is it not better to laugh together as friends?
> Is it not better to sleep quietly at night
> with our wives and our children beside us?

Each day the Ancestors draw me closer to them.
Soon my voice will be silent.
Who then will counsel patience,
when your hogs trample our gardens?
Who then will counsel patience,
when you seize our villages?
Consider the ways of peace,
Coat-wearing people.
You to whom we brought corn,
consider the ways of peace.

"It pleased God to move the
Indians . . . to refresh us . . ."
—Captain John Smith

🎵 A Pilgrim Boy

WILLIAM HOPKINS
Plymouth, England, September 5, 1620

We were cruelly scorned in England
when we wished to have our say
of just how we should worship God
and keep His Sabbath day.
Many families fled to Holland,
a fair—but worldly—nation.
Then our leaders got a patent
to establish a plantation:
a plantation in New England
where we will fish and farm,
where we will follow our own ways
not fearing jail nor harm.

Now we're anchored in the harbor.
On the morning tide, we sail.
It will be a great adventure.
With God's grace we cannot fail!

1620 The *Mayflower* arrives
in Plymouth Bay,
Massachusetts.

". . . regard unto simple truth
in all things."
—William Bradford,
governor of Plymouth Colony

🐛 Speaking of the Pilgrims

CAPTAIN JOHN SMITH
London, England, 1621

I tried to help the Pilgrims,
but their ears were closed to me.
I knew the nature of the land,
the perils of the sea.
I offered to go with them,
to guide them, and to stay.
They did not keep me waiting
before they answered "Nay!"
I warned about the riptides,
the currents, and the shoals.
Such things seemed to be trifles
to these pure and modest souls.
They took no hooks for catching cod,
which was a bad mistake.
I had good advice to give them—
but none that they would take.

"They knew they were
Pilgrims."—William Bradford

1614 Captain John Smith
explores New England.

1619 The first Africans arrive
on a Dutch slave ship and
are exchanged for food
supplies. Like indentured
servants, the Africans are
freed after five years.

1626 The Dutch establish
New Netherland.

1629 The Massachusetts Bay
Colony is founded.

1636 Roger Williams starts the
colony of Rhode Island at
Providence.

4

A Proper Name for a Person

FRANCIS PAYNE
Virginia, 1656

Shucking off old names,
Shucking off old names,
Shucking off old names . . .
I'm free!
I'm free!

Francisco a Negro.
That's what they called me,
when I was Jane Eltonhead's property.
But I bought my freedom,
and I changed my name.
Francisco a Negro
became . . .
Francis Payne.

Shucking off old names,
Shucking off old names,
Shucking off old names . . .
I'm free!
I'm free!

1660 Navigation Act passed
to govern colonial trade.

1664 Slavery Act passed
in Maryland.

1664 English take New
Amsterdam from the Dutch
and rename it New York.

1675–76 King Philip's War
between Indians and white
settlers in New England.

1677 First large group of
Quakers settles in New
Jersey.

🐛 Lessons

PATIENCE and GOODY HANISCH

Keene, New Hampshire, 1687

PATIENCE:

I would someday a goodwife be.

I'll make a cheese to store away!

I would someday a goodwife be.

All of which the Lord will please!

Keep the fires ready to light.

HER MOTHER:

So learn from Mother as you should
to milk the cow, the butter churn,
to separate the curds and whey.

But more important than all these,
all of which the Lord will please:
Tend your hearth attentively.
Keep the fires ready to light.
Let brands smolder day and night.

Make much use of the garden hoe.
Grow turnips, parsnips, cabbage, peas.

But more important than all these:
Tend your hearth attentively.

Keep the fires ready to light.
Let brands smolder day and night.

1680 New Hampshire named a royal colony.

1686 King James II forms the Dominion of New England: New Jersey, New York, Connecticut, Rhode Island, Massachusetts, New Hampshire, Maine.

I would someday a goodwife be.

All of which the Lord will please!

Help card the wool and spin and sew.
Grow flax and dye with indigo.

But more important than all these:

Tend your hearth attentively.
Keep the fires ready to light.

Tend your hearth attentively.
Keep the fires ready to light.
Let brands smolder day and night.

I would someday a goodwife be.

Feed well the pigs and salt the ham.
Turn summer's berries into jam.

All of which the Lord will please!
But more important than all these:
Tend your hearth attentively.
Keep the fires ready to light.
Let brands smolder day and night.

All of which the Lord will please!
But more important than all these:
Tend your hearth attentively.
Keep the fires ready to light.

Let brands smolder day and night.

1689 English troops and Iroquois attack the French in Montreal.

1690 French troops and Algonquin attack settlements in New Hampshire, Maine, and New York.

1692 Twenty witches executed in Salem, Massachusetts.

To Hans in Germany

SOLOMON HESS
Charles Town, South Carolina, December 31, 1699

Oh, the forests! Oh, the trees!
Oh, the land—its boundless quantity!
Jobs and opportunities—so many possibilities!
A new life, a new century—come to these fair colonies!

Oh, the land—its boundless quantity!
Fifty acres to men who sponsor lads like me.
A new life, a new century—come to these fair colonies!
Five years' work and you'll be free.

Fifty acres to men who sponsor lads like me.
My master likes the work I do. Be glad. He'll indenture *you*.
Five years' work and you'll be free.
He'll pay for your crossing (that woeful misery).

My master likes the work I do. Be glad. He'll indenture *you*.
Jobs and opportunities—so many possibilities!
He'll pay for your crossing (that woeful misery).
Oh, the forests! Oh, the trees!

For the Love of William Penn

HANNAH PENN, his widow
Berkshire, England, 1718

The "speedy trip" we took to save our government
became a snare of false claims, jail, torment.
It's been seventeen years since we left Pennsbury.
Seventeen years since the Indians have seen us.
Ah, how they loved William Penn.
Onas, they called him, the Indian word for quill.
How tender of their feelings was Onas.
He dealt with them lovingly,
as blood of his blood—his equals.

Today a wooden case arrived.
For love of Onas
they have sent me animal skins
from which to make a garment:
a garment to protect me from sharp thorns.
        For now I must walk
                alone
            through the wilderness
without Onas as my guide.

"Any government is free
to the people . . ."
—William Penn

❧ Poor Richard's Almanack

TERENCE ROSS, apprentice
Philadelphia, Pennsylvania, 1733

There's never been an almanack
quite like ours, I think.
We bought the very whitest paper
We mixed the very blackest ink.
We took the very greatest care.
We watched our p's.
We watched our q's.
We put in all the information
we know people need to use.
    But . . .
like a cook who makes a pudding
adding raisins and sweet spice,
Mr. Franklin filled *Poor Richard's*
with wise morsels of advice.
Bits that insist on residing
in my mind so I can't stop
        thinking
    of them
        when I leave
            my leather apron
        in this shop.
Bits so useful they're imprinted—
    inked on memory and learned.
    How could anyone forget
    A penny saved; a penny earned?

"Little strokes fell great oaks."—Benjamin Franklin

"Remember that time is money."—Benjamin Franklin

11

My Favorite Time

ELIZABETH BRANDON
Windsor, Connecticut, November 1752

In the evenings after supper,
when all of our chores are done,
our family gathers near the hearth
for some restful, quiet fun.
I helped make the tallow candles.
Now their warm and gentle glow
casts soft light upon my sampler
as I settle down to sew.
In the center winding roses
rise around our cottage door.
Someday they may look just that way,
when they grow a little more.
Mother wove the sturdy homespun;
Father made the willow frame.
And now carefully I'll cross-stitch
the year . . .
and then . . .
my name.

GOD BLESS THIS HOME.
—Sampler message

12

A Meditation

FATHER JUNIPERO SERRA

Mission San Carlos Borromeo del Rio Carmelo, California, July 1771

Bells at sunrise . . .
Bells at sunset . . .
Day by day and year by year.
Bells at sunrise . . .
Bells at sunset . . .
A solemn sweetness in my ear.
As I walk between the missions:
San Diego,
      Monterey . . .
I feel St. Francis walking with me
every step along the way.
It was my boyhood dream to serve him
—a missionary in New Spain.
I never dreamed of founding missions,
one by one to form a chain.
How many thick bricks of adobe?
How many curved red roofing tiles?
How many pairs of well-worn sandals
took these feet how many miles?
How many babies did I baptize?
How many weddings did I bless?
How many souls saved from damnation?
I never counted, I confess.
Bells at sunrise . . .
Bells at sunset . . .
twenty, forty, fifty years . . .
Bells at sunrise . . .
Bells at sunset . . .
became the heartbeats of my ears.

1542 Sailing from Mexico, Spaniards explore the California coast.

1579 Sir Francis Drake claims California for England.

1769 Spanish priests build the first mission in California.

1776 San Francisco is established as a Spanish settlement.

13

A Tea Merchant's Daughter

ABAGAIL SHELTON
Boston, Massachusetts, 1773

My father's in a fury.
    And so are all his friends.
England treats us like we're chattel
    to use for its own ends.
England thinks that we Colonials
    have no right to make choices.
They disregard our envoys.
    English ears can't hear our voices.

Now bankruptcy is facing
    their most precious company.
England wants to save it.
    At what cost?
    Our liberty!
They've cut tea taxes to threepence.
    But what's wrong?
    A monopoly!
Just *their* chosen few are allowed to sell
    British East Indian tea.

Tea merchants like my father
    can buy fine tea from the Dutch.
We don't need tea from England.
    Thank you very much!

A party's planned in Boston.
    Who's coming?
They'll be many.
    Will there be cups of British tea?
Tea, yes!
    But cups . . . NOT ANY.

"Taxation without
representation is tyranny."
—Samuel Adams

1770 The Boston Massacre.

1773 The Boston Tea Party.

"What are the Bostonians
complaining about now?"
"They say the fish in their
harbor all taste of tea."
—Popular saying of the time

14

A Conversation on the Edge of War

AMOS DAVIS and ESTHER GOMEZ
Newport, Rhode Island, September 1774

AMOS DAVIS:

I am a loyal British child,
a subject of the King.
And I would not be otherwise.
No. Not for anything.

ESTHER GOMEZ:

You're a spineless little Tory.
You're as brainless as a flea—
too gutless to want freedom
in a land with liberty!

You're a traitor to your country
without proper loyalties.
You speak of "independence."
We are *British* colonies.

Tax us! Tax us! Please, dear King.
Deny us every right.
But do not be surprised, dear King,
if we're prepared . . .
                    to fight!

"Unite for the common
defense."—Samuel Adams

1775 The Battle of Lexington
and Concord.

"What a glorious morning for
America."—Samuel Adams

15

The Challenge

THOMAS JEFFERSON
Philadelphia, Pennsylvania, June 11, 1776

After being forced to quarter
    British troops who burn and kill,
after Laws were made mere mockeries
    the king could change at will,
after losing every basic right,
    after death and desolation,
it's time that we must choose to be
    a free and sovereign nation.
After Lexington and Concord,
    after Crown Point and Breed's Hill,
the people of America
    have had more than their fill!

Now I have the solemn duty
    to draft a Declaration
making thirteen colonies
    an *independent* nation.
My head must guide my heart and hand,
    as my hand guides this pen,
to write words worthy of a land
    with Justice for all Men.

1776 The Congress adopts the
Declaration of Independence
on July 4.

"We hold these truths to be
self-evident: That all men are
created equal. . . ."
—Thomas Jefferson, *Declaration*

"We have it in our power to
begin the world again."
—Thomas Paine

"These are the times that try
men's souls."
—Thomas Paine

Inauguration Day Thoughts

GEORGE WASHINGTON
New York, New York, April 30, 1789

What a heavy obligation.
I must not betray the trust
of this fledgling little nation.
I must start out right. I must.
The War gave us a common cause.
Now loud voices of dissent
grow sharper than a jaguar's claws
raised to strike in discontent.

I must show by words and actions
how free men resolve their fights.
I must balance all the factions—
calm the zealots for States' rights.
I must set the first example
of what a President should be,
as I walk
        on untrodden ground
with
    no path
                in place
        for
me.

1789 George Washington
becomes the first president
of the United States.

The Story of the Cotton Gin

MRS. NATHANAEL GREENE, widow
Mulberry Grove Plantation, Georgia, 1793

Eli Whitney came to Georgia.
Times were hard and jobs were few.
        I said, "Be my guest."
        He thanked me.
"I'll earn my keep by helping you!"
He found a thousand things to fix
and made them right as rain.
He may have come to study law,
but he brought a mechanic's brain.
Mr. Whitney's fixing skills
gave me cause for admiration.
I laid out this pesky problem,
touching each upland plantation:
        Sea-island cotton from the coast
        has such long and silky thread
        that the prices it is fetching
        keep a slew of workers fed.
        Upland cotton—coarser, shorter—
        isn't nearly half as nice.
        Upland cotton takes *more* labor,
        yet brings only *half* the price.
        Unless produced at less expense,
        upland cotton makes no sense!
        Reckon planting, weeding, hoeing,
        while the cotton crop is growing.
        Add up the hours someone needs
        to free the fibers from the seeds. . . .

Before I had a chance to ask,
Mr. Whitney took on the task:
　　　"I know NO way of avoiding
　　　　　　planting,
　　　　　　　picking,
　　　　　　　　　hoeing weeds,
　　but I'll try to build an engine:
　　a gin for catching cotton seeds."

Imagine fifty pairs of hands
working and working all day.
Then watch one gin and just two hands.
That's Mr. Whitney's way!

"Nothing but the rooting out of
slavery can perpetuate our
union."—George Washington

1797 John Adams becomes the
second president of the
United States.

"People . . . buy cotton, sell
cotton, think cotton, eat cotton,
and dream cotton."
—A foreign visitor

19

At the Edge of the 19th Century

A Memorial Parade

HANNAH BALLARD
Kennebec, Maine, December 31, 1799

The drum rolls will still echo in the coming Century.
Black cloaks, white dresses, black bonnets, long white scarves.
Sixteen girls of sixteen years were we—one for each state.
Black-and-white rosettes pinned to our right shoulders.

Black cloaks, white dresses, black bonnets, long white scarves.
General Washington has died, but the Nation goes forward.
Black-and-white rosettes pinned to our right shoulders.
Militia, lawyers, physicians—all marched behind us.

General Washington is dead, but the Nation must go forward.
"First in war, first in peace, and first in the hearts of his countrymen."
Militia, lawyers, physicians—all marched behind us.
The day was bitter cold but clear—a solemn way to end the year.

"First in war, first in peace, and first in the hearts of his countrymen."
Sixteen girls of sixteen years were we—one for each state.
The day was bitter cold but clear—a solemn way to end the year.
The drum rolls will still echo in the coming Century.

My White House Education

SHARON GILLIGAN

The White House, Washington, D.C., January 1803

The Louisiana Purchase
    took most folks by surprise,
but I saw it in the making
    right before these very eyes.
All those dinners keep us busy,
    but I love my job! It's true.
While serving soup called *consommé*,
    I find out what is new:
What's worrying the President?
What does Congress want to do?

Mr. James Monroe ate fish *filet*,
    before sailing off to France
to give Minister Livingston's mission
    more strength—a better chance.
What was it?
    To buy New Orleans,
    which slick Spain in a secret deal
had ceded back to foxy France.
    And then . . . sought to conceal.

1801 Thomas Jefferson becomes the third president of the United States.

"We are to give money of which we have too little for land of which we have too much."
—Boston Federalist newspaper

Just as I served the *tarte des pommes*,
    the President made mention
that he did not trust Napoleon.
    What was that one's sly intention?
Extending the French Empire
to the West of our young nation!
We'd be forced to turn to Britain.
    What a vexing situation!

"The Constitution fails to say
    if our country has the right
to buy new territories,
    but I'd rather buy than fight!"

"Dear friend," said Mr. James Monroe
    as I filled his cup with tea.
"We can't afford to risk a war.
    On that point, we both agree!"

I never had a chance to learn
    much reading or much writing,
But my White House education
    is ever so exciting!

"I hold it, that a little rebellion, now and then, is a good thing, and as necessary in the political world as storms in the physical."
—Thomas Jefferson

"There is on the globe one single spot . . . New Orleans . . . through which the produce of three eighths of our territory must go to market."
—Thomas Jefferson

A Last-Minute Inventory

MERIWETHER LEWIS
Pittsburgh, Pennsylvania, August 31, 1803

What do I have to take with me?
Mother's wisdom about botany.
　　And her words,
"Observe plants carefully!"
Boyhood skills from the frontier:
ways of oppossum, bear, bird, deer . . .
Tough feet that love to roam and tramp,
tracking, shooting, making camp . . .
Army years where I learned to care:
to take each man's measure fair and square.

24

Plantation duties that gave me command
of all who farmed the family land.
Facts from the President's library,
his lessons on astronomy,
surveying,
and
geography . . .
Advice from the experts who tutored me . . .
and *boundless* curiosity.

My chance to advance humanity
depends on more than bravery!

"I join with you hand and
heart."—William Clark

"Great joy in camp. We are in
view of the ocean."
—William Clark

"Of courage undaunted . . ."
—Thomas Jefferson, describing
Meriwether Lewis

A Seaman's Chantey

SKIPPY McGEE
Aboard the Sea Lion, *1812*

A sailor's life! A sailor's life!
    Now that's the life for me.
I signed aboard a merchant ship
    to sail across the sea.
We left from Savannah—
    stars and stripes strung high.
Climbing up the rigging,
    A happy man was I.

A British ship! A battleship
    with cannon and the Union Jack!
Our captain let the press crew board,
    when facing an attack.
They claimed I was an Englishman,
    and took four mates and me,
although we're all Americans
    as anyone can see.

A sailor's life? A sailor's life?
    This is *no life* for me.
A tar upon a British ship,
    I am no longer free.
And I can only curse the day,
    I chose to go to sea.
And I can only curse the day,
    I chose to go to sea.

1809 James Madison becomes the fourth president of the United States.

1817 James Monroe becomes the fifth president of the United States.

"Oh, say, does that star-spangled banner yet wave . . ."
—Francis Scott Key

26

🌿 The Trail of Tears

BARBARA WANK

near Hopkinsville, Kentucky, February 1839

How long
have they been shuffling
past our cabin
through mud, and sleet,
and now new-fallen snow?
From dawn to dusk
I hear the sad voices of the Cherokees
and the prodding voices of the soldiers,
giving no time for the old and sick to rest
or the dead to be mourned.
Even the darkness
aches with sorrow sound.

1825 John Quincy Adams becomes the sixth president of the United States.

1829 Andrew Jackson becomes the seventh president of the United States.

"In truth, our cause is your own. It is the cause of liberty and justice. . . . We have gloried to count your Washington and your Jefferson as our great teachers. . . ."—Cherokee appeal to Congress

"We were driven off like wolves . . . like wild horses."
—A survivor of the Trail of Tears

Wondering

NOAH SMATHERS
Oregon Territory, August 1843

All I asked was, "Pa, you reckon
    that we're halfway there?"
Pa snarled back like a wild she-bear.
"You ask that question ten times a day!"
(I don't. No, I don't. But I didn't dare say.)

When we left Independence four months ago,
I didn't know time could ever run so slow.
At first it was fun riding up here all day,
seeing new places along the way:
    deserts and prairies,
            a wild river flood
with our wheels cutting ruts through the dust and the mud—
seeing strange critters I've never seen before:
    moose and rattlers,
      buffalo by the score.
Past Laramie, South Pass, then Fort Hall—
through woods so full of giant trees
no sky poked through at all.

1837 Martin van Buren
becomes the eighth president
of the United States.

1841 William Henry Harrison
becomes the ninth president
of the United States.

When we stop for the night, it's
    "Fetch water."
        "Find wood."
    "Rock the baby."
        "Stir the pot."
    "Listen up."
        "Be good."
And *always, always, always,* it's
    "Don't stray away!"
And *never, never, never* is it
    "Run off and play!"

Ma says in Vancouver
    there'll be playing time to spare.
I just wonder what Pa reckons.
    Are we halfway there?

"Our title to . . . Oregon
Territory is clear. . . ."
—James K. Polk

". . . our manifest destiny to
overspread the continent for
our expanding millions."
—John L. O'Sullivan, journalist

1841 John Tyler becomes the
    tenth president of the
    United States.

1845 James K. Polk becomes
    the eleventh president of
    the United States.

29

🌿 Career Plans

ABNER O'LEARY
St. Joseph, Missouri, April 1860

What am I gonna be?
Come on.
Take a guess!
I'm gonna be a rider
for the Pony Express.
I'll hop on a horse
right here in St. Joe.
Like a streak of lightning,
off I'll go!
Riding, riding, riding . . .
fast as can be.
In ten miles
the next guy will take off like me!
Black horse . . .
pinto . . .
chestnut mare . . .
Riding, riding, riding
with no time to spare!
Whizzing past the stagecoach . . .
past the buffalo . . .
Folks no sooner see us coming,
then they'll see us go!

1849 Zachary Taylor becomes the twelfth president of the United States.

Palomino pony . . .
  dapple gray . . .
      Giddy-up!
        Giddy-up!
          Yippee-ki-ay!

        I'll get mail to Sacramento
          in ten days or less,
            when I get to be a rider
              for the Pony Express!

1850 Millard Fillmore becomes
the thirteenth president of
the United States.
        1853 Franklin Pierce becomes
        the fourteenth president of
        the United States.
            1857 James Buchanan
            becomes the fifteenth
            president of the
            United States.

        "Make way for the
        Pony Express!"

Freedom!

HARRIET TUBMAN
Auburn, New York, 1861

Before I rode "The Railroad,"
      I didn't understand.
I thought that tracks were tunneled
      underneath the land.
The Underground Railroad
      runs out of sight.
The last stop is freedom
      if you ride it right.
Good people gave me food
      and hid me all the way,
until I reached Pennsylvania
      at sunrise one day.
I stared at these black hands
      to make sure I was me.
I felt I was in heaven.
      At last I was free!

1861 Abraham Lincoln becomes the sixteenth president of the United States.

"Look for the lantern. Listen for the bell."—Instructions for runaway slaves

I worked as a cook,
        saved my money
            and then . . .
        I went down South
        again and . . . again
to lead others to the stations:
        women, children, men.
Yes, I worked and I saved
        and I kept going back.
I never lost a passenger
        or ran my train off the track.

Folks began to call me Moses.
        The thought tickled me.
Moses! There was a conductor
        who set God's children free.

33

At the Station, Part I

CHARLENE DOOLITTLE
Columbus, Ohio, February 1861

People have been waiting since early in the day.
A train is taking Honest Abe each mile of the way—
All the way from Springfield to Washington, D.C.
President Lincoln! Soon that's who he will be!

With bread and butter sandwiches—Mama in her shawl—
we climbed up a wood pile, being careful not to fall.
"From up here," said Papa, "we're sure to have a view."
We waited, waited, waited while the crowd grew and grew.

I was glad I had that comforter I didn't want to take.
Our bread and butter sandwiches tasted just like cake.
We waited, waited, waited through that chilly afternoon.
Then a distant whistle—Abe's train was coming soon!

As it pulled into the station, brass bands struck up a song.
Marshals tried to clear a way among the cheering throng.
The crowd began to push, to press, to jostle, and to shove.
Papa lifted me so high that I could see Abe from above.

The tall man in a stovepipe hat smiled when he saw me.
President Lincoln!
    Soon that's who he would be.

"The ballot is stronger than
the bullet."
—Abraham Lincoln

"A house divided against
itself cannot stand."
—Abraham Lincoln

A Bird's-Eye View of the Civil War

OLD ABE, THE EAGLE
Madison, Wisconsin, September 1864

I was just an eaglet when the Civil War began,
living as a pet with a man called Dan McCann.
Volunteers were needed to form the infantry.
Dan didn't volunteer himself. He volunteered . . . ME!

The men called me Old Abe, and I've done the best I can
to be a worthy namesake of that brave and honest man.
    Joining the Wisconsin 8th, with my Company,
    I'm carried into battle as their flag flies next to me!
When the bands play marches, I flap and stretch my wings.
But oh, from my high perch, I've seen such *dreadful* things!

Men boasted to each other: "We'll finish this war fast!"
"They're outnumbered three to one." "Johnny Reb won't last."
"We'll be home by Christmas." That's what so many said.
    By Christmas some were wounded.
            By Christmas some were dead.
Through snow,
    through mud,
        through broiling heat,
men march . . .
    and then march more . . .
for the Beast that feasts on human life—
    the Beast called Civil War.

"Atlanta is ours!"
—William T. Sherman,
Union general

"Fourscore and seven years
ago our fathers brought forth
on this continent, a new nation,
conceived in Liberty, and
dedicated to the proposition
that all men are created
equal."—Abraham Lincoln

35

At the Station, Part II

CHARLENE DOOLITTLE
Columbus, Ohio, April 1865

People have been waiting, as night replaces day.
A train is taking Honest Abe each mile of the way—
All the way to Springfield from Washington, D.C.
Rolling back to Illinois . . . and into history.

Bells are tolling, tolling, tolling, while the wheels click-clack.
For miles beyond the station, people wait along the track.
No brass band stands ready to play a marching song.
No one cheers or pushes as the train rolls along.

The crowd is sad and silent. Some weep quietly.
And I cry for the man in a stovepipe hat . . .
        once he smiled at me.

"... malice toward none ...
charity for all."
—Abraham Lincoln

1865 President Lincoln is shot
at Ford's Theater by John
Wilkes Booth and dies at
dawn on April 15.

✤ A Letter to China

KUN-YANG LIN
Sierra Nevada, August 1867

Esteemed Parents:
We hardly know their language—
just their hate and their disgust—
    as we see them sneer
        and we hear them jeer,
keeping silent as we must.

They give us the most dangerous jobs.
Each day we prove our skill.
    They are loud and rough.
        We are quiet . . . but tough,
bending mountains with sheer will.

They never use our proper names.
We're not men to them, I think.
    We don't show our fright.
        We plant dynamite,
making way for the next rail link.

I am so exhausted, Parents.
Too tired this night to sleep.
But at dawn I'll work with honor
for wages that you must keep.

1865 Andrew Johnson becomes
the seventeenth president of
the United States.

37

🐦 A Tie-Tack's Tale

EZRA O'BRIAN
Nebraska, 1868

Rickety-rack! Rickety-rack!
My poppa was a lumberjack.
He gave me his ax.
He showed me a tree.
He said,
"Be a lumberjack like me!"

Rickety-rack! Rickety-rack!
The Union Pacific's laying track.
I picked up Pa's ax.
I found me a tree.
I said,
"You need ties, so buy 'em from me!"

Thirty, forty ties a day.
The Union Pacific's glad to pay.
Rickety-rack! Rickety-rack!
I follow the path of the railroad track.
I swing Pa's ax,
and I cut new wood.
The work is hard,
but the pay is good.

Rickety-rack! Rickety-rack!
They don't call me a lumberjack.
Rickety-rack! Rickety-rack!
I'm a tickety-tackety tie-tack!
A tie-tack?
A tie-tack!
A rickety-rackety tie-tack!
Rickety-rack! Rickety-rack!
A rickety-tickety-rackety-tackety . . .
Tie-tack!

1869 Ulysses S. Grant becomes
the eighteenth president of
the United States.

A Pioneer Woman Looks Back

MARY STAHLER
Kansas, 1874

"Free for the taking. At that price, YOU can buy . . . a garden
in the West . . . endless land and endless sky!"

We were just newlyweds.
John said, "It seems best
to grow with the country—
raise our family out West."
We were young. We were strong.
How were we to know
land and sky could be cruel?
We got ready to go.
I smiled through my tears,
as our loved ones waved good-bye.
We crossed
the Mississippi
for
endless land . . .   endless sky . . .

The trail was rough
and the going was tough.
The prairies of Kansas
were far West enough.
John staked out our claim
one hot day in July,
as I waited and I watched—
endless land . . .   endless sky . . .

Young John was born
early that fall.
Next came Mary,
then Elizabeth . . .
nine kids in all.

I schooled the children.
Town was too far away.
There were so many chores
to fit into a day!
Cooking, sewing, laundry—
and much more to do.
Yet somehow I found time
to be lonely, too:
The endless droning of the wind,
a lone coyote's call,
the chatter of the children,
no visitors at all.
I longed to see a woman—
to hear a woman's voice.
Instead, I hear winds whisper:
Free land! You made a choice.
Often I wonder,
and I can't help but sigh—
What price we really paid
for
endless land . . .   endless sky . . .

"Cheap or free land—clear or
covered with forest."
—Newspaper advertisement

1876 The United States
celebrates its centennial.

"Go west, young man."
—J. B. L. Soule

❦ A Useless Gadget

GARDNER GREEN HUBBARD and **THOMAS SANDERS**
Boston, Massachusetts, May 31, 1875

GARDNER GREEN HUBBARD:

He is such a brilliant fellow—
Alexander Graham Bell.

THOMAS SANDERS:

*But the gadget which intrigues him
sometimes makes that hard to tell.*

I wish he'd do something useful
and leave that thing alone.

*He wastes our money tinkering.
Who needs a telephone?*

"Mr. Watson, come here.
I want you."
—Alexander Graham Bell

1877 Rutherford B. Hayes becomes
the nineteenth president
of the United States.

Thomas Alva Edison: Our Visit

SARAH BERNHARDT
Menlo Park, New Jersey, December 4, 1880

A theatre critic dubbed me
    "Sarah, the Divine."
From Paris to America
    each audience was mine.
Camellias filled my dressing room,
    while outside the stage door
a crush of eager gentlemen
    pressed me to take more.
But there was one American
    whom I wished to meet and see
as much as any of my fans
    might wish to be with me.

So . . .
after taking one last bow
    at my last New York matinee,
I donned a long black hooded cloak
    and quietly slipped away.
It was well after midnight
    when my train reached Menlo Park.
A horse-drawn carriage was waiting.
    Snowflakes swirled in the darkest dark.
Lulled by the wheels, I was dozing.
    Someone shouted, "Hip, hip, hooray!"
Suddenly lights flashed in triumph.
    I awoke to a scene from a play!
Thomas Alva Edison—
    enshrined in his temple of light.

(continued)

"Genius is one percent inspiration and ninety-nine percent perspiration."
—Thomas Edison

"I have not failed. I have just found 10,000 ways that it won't work."—Thomas Edison

Now *I* was the dazzled audience.
      It was Edison's stage that night.
We became the best of friends
      as we toured his laboratories.
At last we reached the phonograph,
      the crown of all his glories.
He recorded "John Brown's Body."
      I spoke lines by Victor Hugo.
Then he sang "Yankee Doodle"
      to close the amazing show.
His family, roused from their warm beds,
      joined us for a light repast.

And now it's after four A.M.
I'm back on the train at last.

44

✦ Will We Be a New State?

LIZZY BONNEVILLE

Laramie, Wyoming Territory, May 7, 1888

We became a Territory
back in 1868.
Now Wyoming's asking Congress
to accept us as a State.
"We won't come in without our women!"
That's the message from Cheyenne.
(To vote in any *other* State,
you *have* to be a man.)

My granny cast a ballot,
almost twenty years ago.
Women judges in Wyoming
show they know what they should know.
When Congress sees our Constitution
in Washington, D.C.,
they will see a plank protecting
voting rights for Ma and me.
That could cause a royal rumpus
and a whirlwind of debate.
But . . .
if they won't let our women vote,
Wyoming *won't* become a State.

1881 Chester A. Arthur
becomes the twenty-first
president of the
United States.

1885 Grover Cleveland
becomes the twenty-second
president of the United
States.

🌾 A Matter of Life or . . . Death

JAKE KAHN
Chicago, Illinois, 1893

Mama, Papa, I'll *die* if we don't go.
We *have* to see
Bill Cody's Wild West Show!
Folks say that you've
never
ever
really had a thrill
until you've seen the likes
of Buffalo Bill.
Annie Oakley, Little Sure Shot—
she's sure to be there—
putting holes through playing cards
tossed up in the air!
Forty, fifty cowboys—daredevils all—
ride faster than tornadoes
and NEVER take a fall!
Arapaho, Shoshone, chiefs of the Sioux,
calf ropers, bulldoggers—
they'll be there, too!
The Deadwood Stagecoach,
the Pony Express . . .
You want to see them.
Don't you? Confess!
With thousands of seats, the tickets don't last.
We better get there fast, fast, fast!
Mama, Papa, I'll *die* if we don't go.
We *have* to see
Bill Cody's Wild West Show!

"Home, home on the
range . . ."—Cowboy song

Don't Forget Us!

ANNIE McDOUGAL
Perry, Oklahoma, 1894

They call me Cattle Annie
for the rustling that I do.
Little Britches, she's my partner,
is a darn good rustler, too.
You won't find sharper horse thieves
in all of the Southwest.
But robbing banks with the Wild Bunch—
that's what we like the best!
When those marshals finally caught us,
Little Britches got away.
They shot her horse from under her.
We were sentenced yesterday.
Gunmen get all the glory—
The Dalton Gang and Jesse James.
When we're in the reformatory,
please, don't forget our names!
We never got to rob a train.
That's a thing that we both regret.
But I've promised Little Britches
that we'll do it someday yet!

1893 Grover Cleveland
becomes the twenty-fourth
president of the United
States.

A Gold Miner's Tale

FRANK WEXLER
Dawson City, Yukon Territory, 1898

I was twenty-one years old.
    Fired up by dreams of gold.
      Rushing West in '49
        to stake a claim to my own mine!
          What did I find when I got there?
            Thousands of "rushers" everywhere!
   Water and sand. That's ALL it takes.
   Swish your pan. Pick out the flakes!

A meal?
    A horse?
      A place to stay?
Who'd believe what we had to pay!

Bought a shovel. Bought a pan.
Soon I'd be a rich young man.
    Water and sand. That's ALL it takes.
    Swish your pan. Pick out the flakes!
Pan after pan, I'd swish and wish
for a glint of pay dirt in my dish.
Asleep at night, what did I see?
Nuggets the daylight hid from me.
It takes more than a flash in the pan
to make a rusher a rich young man.

The gold I found? Just enough to get by.
I gave up when my claim went dry.
        Water and sand. That's ALL it takes.
        Swish your pan. Pick out the flakes!
Got a job in a hydraulic mine.
Hated the work, but the pay was fine.
So when I heard about Pikes Peak,
        I
            was
                in
                    the Rockies
                        within a week!

        Water and sand. That's ALL it takes.
        Swish your pan. Pick out the flakes!
I should have known better.
        With a grubstake so small,
        I left Colorado with nothing at all.
No job. No gold. Just a shovel and a pan.
        But I walked away a wiser man.

"Gold in the Klondike!"
        Wouldn't you think
        I'd be up there in a wink?
But with my new plan to pan gold flakes,
I didn't make the same mistakes.
Before I joined the great stampede,
I thought: What will stampeders need?
Now I'm a Dawson millionaire!
I sell them ALL long underwear.

GOLD BONANZA IN COLORADO.
—Newspaper headline

PIKES PEAK OR BUST!
—Prospector's sign

BUSTED AT PIKES PEAK
—Failed prospector's sign

At the Edge of the 20th Century

A Modern Girl

NANCY POTAK
Minneapolis, Minnesota, December 31, 1899

Farewell, 19th Century!
The future calls my friends and me.
Our Eastman Kodaks click, click, click.
We take snapshots quick, quick, quick!

The future calls my friends and me.
What new wonders will we see?
We take snapshots quick, quick, quick!
We don't want to miss a trick.

What new wonders will we see?
Telephones, electric lights: we're ready for fantastic sights.
We don't want to miss a trick.
Trolleys, subways, submarines, Ferris wheels—such grand machines!

Telephones, electric lights: we're ready for fantastic sights.
Our Eastman Kodaks click, click, click.
Trolleys, subways, submarines, Ferris wheels—such grand machines!
Farewell, 19th Century!

✈ The First Airplane

ORVILLE and WILBUR WRIGHT
Kitty Hawk, North Carolina, 1903

I'm Orville.

I'm younger.

Two brothers.
One team.
We both loved mechanics.
Even as boys
we made pocket money

And always one question:
What makes it tick?

Then we worked together.
Two brothers.
One team.
Bicycle builders

Our minds seemed to fit
like a set of oiled gears.
When I caught typhus,

We grew even closer,
Perhaps that is why
we *both* were possessed.
Two brothers
One vision

I'm Wilbur.

I'm older.
Two brothers.
One team.
We both loved mechanics.
Even as boys

by inventing toys.
And always one question:
What makes it tick?

Then we worked together.
Two brothers.
One team.

Self-taught engineers
Our minds seemed to fit
like a set of oiled gears.

I feared you might die.
We grew even closer,

we both were possessed.

One vision

One quest:
A machine to defy

A machine with control

to fly!
A machine that was light

A mechanical puzzle
with the question we share:
What makes it tick?
I'm Orville.

Two bodies.
One mind.
Thoughts merging

new answers
to find.
Building gliders

not resting
just testing
and testing and testing . . .
and testing and testing . . .
designing . . .

rethinking . . .

Then building the Flyer
exactly to plan
and knowing *for certain*

Two brothers
One quest:

the whims of the sky.

and the power
to fly!

but weighed more than air.
A mechanical puzzle
with the question we share:
What makes it tick?

I'm Wilbur.
Two bodies.
One mind.

thoughts meshing
new answers
to find.

becoming sky riders

just testing
and testing and testing . . .
and testing and testing . . .

combining . . .

refining . . .
Then building the Flyer
exactly to plan
and knowing for certain

(continued)

53

it would carry . . .
a man!
And we were . . .
both right.
Yes, we were
Wright!
I'm Orville.

Two brothers.
One team.
I'm Orville.

Two brothers.
One dream.

it would carry . . .
a man!
And we were . . .
both Wright.
Yes, we were
right!

I'm Wilbur.
Two brothers.
One team.

I'm Wilbur.
Two brothers.
One dream.

"They'll never make a
machine that will fly."
—The Wrights' neighbors

"Success. Four flights
Thursday morning."
—Orville and Wilbur Wright

⚏ A Letter to Kermit

PRESIDENT THEODORE ROOSEVELT
The White House, Washington, D.C., June 21, 1904

Blessed Son,
            I feel so very fortunate to be the President.
We love living in the White House. Your mother is content.
Not every man can do the work that he knows should be done.
I'm lucky I've accomplished my objectives one by one:
      The Panama Canal—now won't it be terrific?—
      uniting, as it will, the Atlantic and Pacific.
      The virgin forests that I've saved from certain devastation
      will be a living heritage for future generations.
      A square deal for the working man won't harm the millionaire.
      And if we must, let's bust a trust! Business should play fair.
I've tried to install honesty "from shore to shining shore."
I'm thankful to have had this chance, and I'd like four years more.
Will I be nominated at the Republican Convention?
Some grumble I'm progressive, yet there's no one else they mention.
How will national elections go? It's much too soon to tell.
If I lose, I won't be sour,
      but if I win—won't that be swell?
Your loving father

1901 President McKinley is assassinated in Buffalo, New York.

1901 Theodore Roosevelt becomes the twenty-sixth president of the United States.

"Speak softly and carry a big stick."—Theodore Roosevelt

55

⚑ America!

FANYA ALBERT
Ellis Island, New York, March 7, 1911

Soon the Golden Land would welcome them,
the first-class passengers,
the ones with cabins.
From behind the metal gate
I could glimpse fragments:
  a billowing feather on a hat,
 a silk scarf,
    a tapered hand in pale suede,
  an elegant carrying case.
They would go straight to the city.

Not us. Not the steerage.
  Feathers?
Ours, if any, had been sewn into quilts.
We had no suede gloves,
  no silk—
just babushkas and bundles,
hopes and prayers.
First we must go to Ellis Island.

We waited.
A human jumble:
babies crying, elders sighing,
our ears swimming in a noisy stew:
German, Italian, Swedish, Yiddish,
even English with an Irish lilt.
We did not understand each others' words,
except one,
        America!

At last the gate swung open,
and we crowded onto the ferry.
Then, as it pulled away from the ship,
we saw her—Lady Liberty!
A goddess
rising from the sea,
her strong arm holding a torch
as if to light our way.
One by one we whispered the word,
        "America!"
                "America!"
Again and again,
                        "America!"
        "America!"
until
        the echoed word became a blizzard!
A swarm of sparkling jewels that *I* could see
                hovering
        over the dark water.

A Song for Suffrage

VIRGINIA BURTON

Wilmington, Delaware, February 1913

We are marching, marching, marching
    off to Washington, D.C.,
With a message for the President,
    whom we intend to see.
Men claim that they adore us!
    "Voting would be such a strain."
So we're marching, marching, marching,
    but we might melt in the rain!

Chorus: Women, we've been told it's fitting
    to stay home and do our knitting.
    But we're determined. We're not quitting.
    Won't you march with us today?

We're soldiers in the Women's Army.
    Sisters, come along, enlist.
We'll never get the right to vote
    unless we all insist.
You can march with us for one mile.
    You can march with us for ten.
As we march to the Potomac
    for the right to vote like men!

1913 Woodrow Wilson becomes
the twenty-eighth president
of the United States.

Chorus: Women, we've been told it's fitting
          to stay home and do our knitting.
          But we're determined. We're not quitting.
          Won't you march with us today?

Men say they wish to protect us
          and proceed to show us how.
They can take away our children
          the way laws are written now.
They are ready to protect us
          from our fathers' tyranny
By controlling what Dad leaves us
          to make sure we're worry-free!

Chorus: Women, we've been told it's fitting
          to stay home and do our knitting.
          But we're determined. We're not quitting.
          Won't you march with us today?

"And ain't I a woman?"
—Sojourner Truth

"We hold these truths to be
self-evident; that all men and
women are created equal. . . ."
—Elizabeth Cady Stanton

MR. PRESIDENT,
WHAT WILL YOU DO
FOR SUFFRAGE?
—Banner held outside
the White House by two
suffragettes for a year, 1917.

⚑ The Assembly Line

BILLY BERMAN
Highland Park, Michigan, January 1914

Five dollars a day!
    Five dollars a day!
Mr. Ford went and doubled
    my papa's pay!
What's more, on the Ford
    assembly line,
the hours are cut back
    to eight from nine!
Papa used to complain all that he got to do

               is
               stand
               in
               one
               place
               and
               tighten
               one
               screw.

        Day
        after
        day
        from
        morning
       to
        night
      on
car after car the same screw to make tight.

"We're putting together the Model T,
but the screw I turn is all I see.
Each man works in such little bits.
Soon all of us will lose our wits!
The belt speeds up. We work faster and faster.
Are we still men, when Time's our master?"

But now that he's getting twice the pay,
    here's what I hear Papa say:
    Five dollars a day!
      Five dollars a day!
        The
          a
            s
              s
                e
                  m
                  b
                  l
                    y
                      l
                      i
                      n
                      e
                        is here to stay!

"A car for the great
multitude."—Henry Ford

61

Thoughts After the Great War

JANET O'FAOLÁIN and PAOLA SAUNDERS
Olympia, Washington, 1920

JANET:
What won Wilson four years more?

Then what did he say our mission
should be?

What did the Yanks get for thanks?

A hundred thousand brave young
men will never see their homes again.
Trenches, mud and mustard gas . . .
A hundred thousand men, alas!

"A League of Nations . . . "
he *now* supposes.

"Vivez Wilson!"
crowds cheer in France.
A "League of Nations"?
Don't take a chance!

A hundred thousand brave young
men will never see their homes again.

PAOLA:

They claimed, "He kept us out of war."

*Make "the world . . . safe for
democracy."*

*Minefields, rifles, grenades, bombs,
tanks.*

*A hundred thousand brave young
men will never see their homes again.*

A hundred thousand men, alas!

*"A new world order . . . " he now
proposes.*

*A "League of Nations"?
Don't take a chance!*

*A hundred thousand brave young
men will never see their homes again.*

Keeping Cool with Coolidge

PAT LEWIS
Wall Street, New York, New York, 1927

While I shine the big shots' shoes,
I hear all the latest news
Directly from the experts' lips:
bankers'—
      brokers'—
red-hot tips.
Which stocks to buy.
Which stocks to sell.
Ask me.
I'll be glad to tell.

Rich folks have their problems, too.
But not the same as me and you.
It's terrible when you can't decide
which horse to have which jockey ride
or whom to invite on your yacht.
Now that would bother me a lot.
If my son was a fool for flirts
who danced the Charleston in short skirts,
I'm not sure *I'd* sleep well at night,
but there are *some* things I'd get right:
Which stocks to buy.
Which stocks to sell.
Ask me.
I'll be glad to tell.

1921 Warren G. Harding becomes the twenty-ninth president of the United States.

1923 Calvin Coolidge becomes the thirtieth president of the United States.

"The business of America is business."—Calvin Coolidge

1929 Herbert Hoover becomes the thirty-first president of the United States.

"In no nation are the fruits of accomplishment more secure."—Herbert Hoover

Skyscraper

WILLIAM VAN ALEN
New York, New York, 1930

64

With
a frame
of steel
and
a
window
wall
I'll
grow
a
building
strong
and
tall.
Let
it
pierce
the
city
sky.
Clouds don't charge
for
floating
by.
Unseen
an
elevator
spine
rises
in
a
steady
line.
I watch this building
and I feel
I hear it
singing
songs in steel.

A New Deal: That's What the Country Needs

FRANKLIN DELANO ROOSEVELT
Chicago, Illinois, July 1932

The people I call Americans,
Hoover calls "the mob."
Can this be democracy?
The people are no mob to me.
I have met them face to face:
        the factory worker,
        the farmer,
        the miner,
        the veteran,
        the woman, so lean, so worried,
        the hungry children
        whose schools have been closed,
        the elderly
        with fear in their eyes.
They are the forgotten Americans,
the ones without the cards it takes to win.
So let us shuffle the deck
and restore their country to its own people
with . . .
        a new deal.

"A chip off the block that gave
us Teddy. . . ."—Campaign song

1933 Franklin Delano Roosevelt
becomes the thirty-second
president of the
United States.

"This great nation will
endure . . . the only thing we
have to fear is fear itself. . . ."
—Franklin Delano Roosevelt

65

On the Way to Californ-I-A!

EVERETT DANSBY
Mother Road, Oklahoma, 1938

Year after year, the land was dry.
We prayed for rain,
watched crops shrivel and die.
Then the winds started blowing,
and the sky turned bloodred.
But no raindrops fell.
It rained red dust instead.
The sun disappeared.
Day turned into night.
We rushed inside.
Tried to make the house tight.
And the terror winds blew and blew and blew.
And the terror winds blew and blew.

"There's jobs in Californ-I-A!"
That's what Pa says some folks say.
So we loaded our jalopy,
and we're on our way today!
On our way to Californ-I-A
where
oranges,
tomatoes,
and potatoes grow,
and where
terror winds don't *ever* blow.
No, the terror winds don't blow.

"... the whirlwind by day
and the darkness at noon."
—Old Testament

66

▛▟ Shopping

LIZA CHARLESWORTH
Altoona, Iowa, 1940

Five pennies make a nickel.
  Two nickels make a dime.
A dime can buy a treasure
  at Woolworth's every time.
Silk and velvet ribbons . . .
  a tortoiseshell barrette . . .
    perfume for my mother . . .
      a watercolor set . . .
    a whirling, twirling pinwheel . . .
 jacks . . .
a ruby ring . . .
I study every counter
  before I choose a thing.
A hankie with the letter "L"
  the way I start my name . . .
    new crayons . . .
      jigsaw puzzles . . .
      a ball-and-paddle game . . .
If I only had permission,
  my dime could buy a pet:
    a tiny painted turtle . . .
 goldfish scooped up with a net . . .
But sometimes,
  only sometimes,
I save my dime
  and then . . .
I think of how I'll spend it,
  when I come back again.

SHOP 'TIL YOU DROP!
—Bumper sticker

On the Home Front

GINA SHAW
San Antonio, Texas, September 1942

Victor Frager's wearing silver wings.
      Walter Dodge is a marine.
Cousin Sonny's in the army
      with a rifle to keep clean.
Tony Vacca joined the navy.
      Steve Smith's in the Signal Corps.
Jane Finnegan's become a WAC.
      The whole world is at war.

We're busy on the home front,
      doing all that we can do.
We save every bit of tinfoil
      from each stick of gum we chew.
Like our rubber-band collection,
      it gets added to a ball.
Our school principal has told us,
      "The war effort needs it all."
During art class we're all knitting
      squares that someone else will sew
into blankets that are shipped off
      to wherever they should go.
During English we write letters
      so that GIs know we care.
How we feel their boundless courage,
      while we're singing "Over There!"

Neighbors work in Victory Gardens
        in backyards along our street.
We have books of ration coupons
        to buy butter, sugar, meat.
Every evening my whole family
        sits close to the radio.
Are the Allied troops advancing?
        What's the news? We *have* to know.

Uncle Sam peers down from posters,
        and he's saying, "I need you!"
I wish that I knew something else
        that I could *really* do.
Watching newsreels at the movies,
        how I wish I could do more!
And I wonder—Will peace *ever* come?
        The whole world is at war.

"Air raid on Pearl Harbor. This
is no drill."—Telegram from the
commander in chief of the
Pacific fleet.

"A date which will live in
infamy."—Franklin Delano
Roosevelt

"We did it before, and we
can do it again!"
—Popular song

At the Gila River Camp

ROY KATO
Poston, Arizona, 1943

"*G*aman," said *Obesan,* my grandmother.
It means "be brave." Don't cry. Be strong.
"*Gaman,*" she'd say
when my roller skates
sent me sprawling
to the sidewalk
or
when my kitten
dashed beneath a passing car.
Gaman—the word could push back tears
so that they fell inside
where no one could see.

"*Gaman,*" said *Obesan* after Pearl Harbor.
She was a Japanese alien.
And the rest of the family,
we were no longer called Americans.
We were "non-aliens"—
a new way to say "citizens."
And for our protection,
Japanese aliens and non-aliens
must be relocated.

"Gaman," said *Obesan.*
We had four days to sell our house,
Papa's truck, Mama's piano, my red bicycle—
We could only take what we could carry.

Good-bye school,
     good-bye friends,
          good-bye freedom.

For our protection
     our whole family lives in one room.
For our protection
     barbwire surrounds this camp.
For our protection
     the soldiers do not point their guns outside.
For our protection
     they point their guns at us.

"Gaman," says *Obesan.*
"Gaman . . . "

"We have not found a single
gun . . . or a single
camera . . . we believe was
for espionage."—F.B.I.

1945 Harry S. Truman becomes
     the thirty-third president of
     the United States.

The United Nations

ELEANOR ROOSEVELT
Hyde Park, New York, 1947

I hear Franklin's words, although he's at rest.
"Don't discard the good, when you can't have the best."

The President said, "Be my eyes and my ears."
I looked and I listened for so many years.
I brought the pulse of the nation to our partnership
with what I saw and I heard on each fact-finding trip.

"Peace," Franklin said, "will need help to endure.
Peace needs a structure. Of that I am sure."
The United Nations, he thought, could be the way
to work toward world justice and keep war at bay.

I hear Franklin's words, although he's at rest.
"Don't discard the good, when you can't have the best."

Now atomic bombs pose a dark new threat.
The need for peace grows more urgent, yet
the United Nations, it's clear to me,
will be as strong as its members allow it to be.

I hear Franklin's words, although he's at rest.
"Don't discard the good, when you can't have the best."

"We the peoples of the
United Nations determined to
save succeeding generations
from the scourge of war, which
twice in our lifetime has
brought untold sorrow to
mankind . . ."
—Preamble to the charter of
the United Nations

"First Lady of the world."
—President Truman, about
Eleanor Roosevelt

Speaking Up at the Miners' Meeting

JUAN LOPES, LUIS SANCHEZ,
JORGE TORRES, and FELIPE MORALES
Zinctown, New Mexico, 1953

Down in the mines where day is night,
a single man plants dynamite.
What do they care if we get hurt?
Mexican lives are cheap as dirt.

What do the Anglo bosses say
when Anglo miners want more pay?
"Look how much better things are for you.
The Mexican miners make less than you do."

Es verdad. It's true.
Anglos get more money for the same work we do.
Es verdad. It's true.
Anglos do dangerous jobs in pairs of two.

Not so many years ago, this arroyo was in Mexico.
Now we're citizens of the U.S.A.
We want equal conditions! We want equal pay!

¡La verdad es verdad!
¡Queremos igualdad!
¡La verdad es verdad!
¡Queremos igualdad!

"We are fighting for
recognition . . . which is
the real guts of it."
—César Chávez

73

What Do You Think of President Eisenhower?

CHRIS FARLEKAS, roving reporter
Seattle, Washington, June 15, 1959

He let those Nazis know the score.
I liked the way he won the war.
I like Ike!   **Carl Reich, stockbroker**

 I like his easy, honest grin.
 Of course, the voters swept him in!
 I like Ike!   **Diane Zeines, college student**

 In my two-tone four-door car
 I'm the King of France! I'm a Russian czar!
 I like my job. I like my pay.
 Like everybody else, I'll say
 I like Ike!   **Larry Grover, aircraft worker**

 I love the King of Rock and Roll.
 Elvis rules my heart and soul.
 The President? Yes, I confess.
 All that I can do is guess.
 I like Ike!   **Pat Penn, 10th grade**

Our brand-new ranch house is just grand.
I like the picture window and
     the breezeway and
          the kitchen and the carport . . . and . . .
               I like Ike!   **Nancy Wright, housewife**

I'm not quite sure just what Ike meant
by "the military-industrial establishment."
He's got the country running good.
We lead the world as well we should.
He'll know how to strut our stuff
if those Commies start playing rough.
I like Ike!   **Steve Smith, engineer**

I take the wife and kids and go
to the drive-in for a picture show.
A double feature—the kids are free—
all I pay for is the wife and me.
I like Ike!   **Allen Schupinski, carpenter**

A blender,
        a freezer,
                plastic flowers,
TV to watch for hours and hours!
"I Love Lucy"
        but . . .
I like Ike!   **Elsie Plotkin, retired**

I sleep much better now I know
my children won't catch polio.
Dr. Salk, I thank you. So . . .
I like Ike!   **Mariko Sakemi, housewife**

My hula hoop can really whirl.
It makes me glad to be a girl.
My little brother is a brat!
Who wants his Davy Crockett hat?
I hate boys, and that is that, but . . .
I like Ike!   **Jane Yett, 5th grade**

"See the USA in a Chevrolet"
—Theme song for the
Dinah Shore Show

"Mob rule cannot . . . override
our courts."
—Dwight D. Eisenhower

"Now, on Friday noon, I am to
become a private citizen. I am
proud to do so. I look forward
to it."—President Eisenhower's
farewell address

𝖩𝖿 On the Bus

SALLY MAE ROGERS
Washington, D.C., August 28, 1963

Even as it just began
and had not happened yet,
I knew this day would be a day
I never would forget:
 A tuck-away day.
 A remember-when day.
 A day to replay and replay and replay!

In the still of the night
we climbed into the bus.
All over the country
folks were riding like us.
Black folks, white folks, kids like me—
Rolling . . . rolling . . . to Washington, D.C.!

We closed our eyes,
but not for too long!
As we rode out of town,
someone started a song.
We all sang "Oh, Freedom!"
and "We Shall Overcome."
Then a silence fell over everyone.
The words in those songs so strong, so deep
played on in my head when I tried to sleep.

1961 John Fitzgerald Kennedy
 becomes the thirty-fifth
 president of the
 United States.

 "And so, my fellow
 Americans, ask not what
 your country can do for you;
 ask what you can do for
 your country."
 —John F. Kennedy

"Segregated schools are not
equal and cannot be made
equal . . ."—Supreme Court

"I draw the line in the dust and
toss the gauntlet before the
feet of tyranny and I say,
Segregation now! Segregation
tomorrow! Segregation forever!"
—Governor of Alabama
George Wallace

As sunrise spread across the skies,
streams of buses met our eyes.
        Buses passing side by side!
        People on a freedom ride!
Strangers waving to each other.
        Hello, sister! Hello, brother!
Black folks, white folks, kids like me—
Rolling . . . rolling . . . to Washington, D.C.!

When at last we all were there,
a joyful something filled the air.
A sense of hope, a sense of power.
This was surely freedom's hour!

        We marched toward Washington Monument,
            the center of the great event.
            More people than I've ever seen
            gathered there upon the green
        to hear leaders speak and singers sing . . .
        Then there he was—Martin Luther King.
        The words he spoke rang out like a hymn
            and carried us all along with him.
            "I have a dream today," he said.
            " . . . I have a dream today . . . "
                As he painted his dream,
                    we all could see
                a world of love, of dignity,
                of freedom and equality.

Now I'm bringing his dream home with me.
A dream to be my tuck-away.
A dream to replay and replay and replay.
A dream to bring closer day by day.

President Kennedy

SUSAN NOBEL
Nebraska, November 1963

"President Kennedy has been shot in Dallas."
The words did not seem real.
Slowly we began to feel their heaviness
the way you feel the weight of snow,
its cold quiet chill,
before a blizzard.
Our teacher did not try to teach
and even Norman-Know-It-All
had nothing to say.
And then the teacher called us to the window.
Outside the janitor was lowering the flag,
until it flew at half-mast.
We knew that the President had died
And oh, the terrible heaviness and the chill.

1963 President John F. Kennedy is assassinated in Dallas, Texas.

"He gave the country back its best self."
—Arthur Schlesinger, Jr.

1963 Lyndon B. Johnson becomes the thirty-sixth president of the United States.

1968 Dr. Martin Luther King, Jr., is assassinated in Memphis, Tennessee.

The Moondust Footprint

JOSHUA KATZ
Woodstock, Vermont, July 20, 1969

We'd been watching, watching, watching
all day long into the night:
    Mission Control in Houston,
        Apollo astronauts in flight.
A new chapter of history
    was about to open soon.
The Apollo slowed . . . then quickened,
speeding closer to the moon.

The others went to bed,
but not Aunt Mary and me.
We kept watching, watching, watching
    each slow stage on the TV:
        the hovering Landing Module,
            the Sea of Tranquillity,
                and the astronaut, Neil Armstrong,
                    moving oh so carefully . . .
I was holding my breath
    —Aunt Mary said she'd held hers, too—
until we saw the moondust footprint
    made by Armstrong's ribbed left shoe!

That footprint marked a moment—
    an awesome human victory.
We were watching history happen,
    my aunt Mary . . . and me.

"Houston, Tranquillity Base
here. The Eagle has landed."
—Neil Armstrong

"No single space project will
be more impressive. . . ."
—John F. Kennedy,
speaking to Congress

"Zero-G and I feel fine."
—John Glenn

"That's one small step for man,
one giant leap for mankind."
—Neil Armstrong

⊞ The President's Rap, Part I

POLITICAL PULSE, rap artist
Los Angeles, California, 1983

After the death of J.F.K.
who was the President?
L.B.J.! Yes . . .
Lyndon Baines Johnson
decided that he
would create
    the Great
    Society
    and wage
    a War
    on Poverty.
Johnson had the skill
    to muster
    votes to stop
    a filibuster.
He went to Congress
    on the Hill
    and at last
    they passed
the Civil Rights bill.

"My fellow Americans: I am about to sign into law the Civil Rights Act of 1964."
—Lyndon B. Johnson

"Education is the key to the great society."
—Lyndon B. Johnson

"Our goal is peace in Southeast Asia. That will come only when aggressors leave their neighbors in peace."
—Lyndon B. Johnson

80

Richard Nixon
took the oath.
Student protests
grew.
He asked
Henry Kissinger
what to do.
"I've just invented
détente
to be your policy.
A 'man of peace'
is what the world will
see.
We're booked for
China,
but hedge your bets.
Get buddy-buddy
with the Soviets."
America watched.
Nixon looked great.
Then came the
scandal
called Watergate.

1969 Richard M. Nixon
becomes the thirty-seventh
president of the
United States.

"I hereby resign this office of
President of the United
States."—Richard M. Nixon,
August 9, 1974

Vietnam: Are We Winning?

TONY PARISI

Baltimore, Maryland, 1970

My brother Angelo's a Green Beret.
Our family pays attention to TV.
It's not some stranger's war we see.
One of those guys could be Angie.
It could be Angie in one of those places:
Tet, Saigon, Hanoi, My Lai, the Mekong Delta . . .
Soldiers slogging through the jungle.
Choppers churning, villages burning,
the rat-a-tat of gunfire and the sizzle of flares.
Those thin people running in their rice fields.
They're supposed to be the enemy. But why?
We're winning, aren't we? Are we winning?

WAR IS NOT HEALTHY
FOR CHILDREN AND
OTHER LIVING THINGS.
—Bumper sticker

"No event in American history
is more misunderstood than
the Vietnam War."
—Richard M. Nixon

"Yes!" say the generals on TV.
A girl with long dark hair is singing
"Give Peace a Chance."
"There is," says a politician, "a credibility gap."
Protesters are marching, chanting . . .
Who can we believe?
Are we winning?
Are *they* winning?

IN HONOR OF THE MEN AND
WOMEN OF THE ARMED FORCES
OF THE UNITED STATES WHO
SERVED IN THE VIETNAM WAR.
THE NAMES OF THOSE WHO
GAVE THEIR LIVES AND THOSE
WHO REMAIN MISSING ARE
INSCRIBED IN THE ORDER THEY
WERE TAKEN FROM US.
—Vietnam Veterans Memorial,
Washington, D.C.

⚏ The Presidents' Rap, Part II

POLITICAL PULSE, rap artist
Los Angeles, California, 1983

Gerald Ford
took office
after Nixon's resignation.
Unemployment grew
as fast as inflation.

Then . . .
Jimmy Carter
      came in
with a stop-inflation plan.
   But he couldn't stop
      extremists
         in Iran.
The U.S. Embassy was occupied.
      52 hostages
      were locked inside.
"Gimme, gimme," said Jimmy,
   "those hostages back.
Concentrate on your war with Iraq."
      But Iran held out
   on the hostages' release
      until Jimmy Carter
         lost
his White House lease.

1974 Gerald R. Ford becomes
   the thirty-eighth president
   of the United States.

1976 The nation celebrates
   its bicentennial.

"I am a Ford, not a Lincoln."
—Gerald Ford

1977 James Earl Carter
   becomes the thirty-ninth
   president of the
   United States.

"I will never lie to you."
—Jimmy Carter

Now . . .
  Ronald Reagan
  is our Prez.
  "I'll shrink
the government!"
That's what he says.
Tax breaks for the rich
  are gonna
  "trickle down"
  to folks
living on sidewalks
  all over town.
The budget deficit
  gets
bigger and bigger.
What's trickling down?
  It's
hard to figure.

For the Earth Day Essay Contest

JEANETTE NEFF
Aurora, Colorado, April 22, 1970

Someday there may be no "away"
to throw stuff anymore,
so we better all start thinking
and we better know the score.
We better ask some questions
about the things we choose:
Do we want a certain something
to use

      and use

           and use?
When it's broken, small, or empty,
will that be that something's end?

"The Earth does not belong
to the People. The People
belong to the Earth."
—Chief Pontiac

Can we fix it?
        Can we fill it?
                Can we give it to a friend?
Can we make that something something else
        or will that something be
                just a use-it-one-time-toss-it-out,
                    a trash-it—1-2-3?
The garbage trucks
                roll
                        down
                            the streets
when it is garbage day.
But where will they be rolling to
when there is no "away"?

At the Senior Citizens' Political Forum

PEGGY SHAPIRO

Sans Souci Senior Village, Boca Raton, Florida, 1984

Support the Rainbow Coalition!
It's how we can begin
to show we don't judge people
by the color of their skin.
If we had a President
whose words and actions heal
and he was plaid with polka dots,
we'd *still* have a good deal.
Jesse Jackson has a heart,
but he also has a brain.
He's willing to admit mistakes.
So forgive him. Why complain?
"Don't vote and the choice is theirs."
That's the American way.
Even if Jesse's not your man,
don't stay home on Primary Day.

"I am somebody. I may be poor, but I am somebody. . . . Respect me. Protect me. Never neglect me. I am somebody."—Jesse Jackson

"Our flag is red, white and blue, but our nation is a rainbow—red, yellow, brown, black and white—and we're all precious in God's sight." —Jesse Jackson

🐾 Green Card Fever

NEW AMERICANS
Coast to Coast, 1995

We come from
            Haiti,
                    Nevis,
                            Pakistan,
                    India,
                            Afghanistan—
                            Romania,
                    El Salvador,
            China,
        Cuba,
Ecuador—
        Ghana,
            Mali,
                    Katmandu—
                    the Philippines,
                            St. Kitts,
                                    Peru—
                                        Thailand,
                                            Israel,
                                                    Palestine,
                                            Turkey,
                                        Greece,
                                    the Levantine—
                            Guatemala,
                    Mexico . . .

            We ALL know where we want to go!
            Working, striving, trying hard—
                where life depends on a
                GREEN CARD!

"The question is not when we came here . . . but why our families came here. And what we did after we arrived."
—Jimmy Carter

89

A Question to the Youth of America

PRESIDENT BILL CLINTON
Washington, D.C., November 1, 1999

What changes do you think there'll be
in the brand-new century?
Please e-mail me your answers:
president@whitehouse.gov
Then I'll post a folder
with your thoughts re the above.

From ravi@hook.up
Every kid will have a robot
that will get the answers right
for the homework the kid feeds it
after supper every night.

From lori@ecoexplor.net
We won't cut down trees for paper.
The ozone layer will be fine.
Global warming will be history.
We'll read all our words online.

From Mel@palm.com
Before long probably moms and dads will make a careful list
to get the kid they *really* want from some geneticist.
The problems our folks have with us will simply disappear,
when kids are made to order by a genetic engineer.

From eduardo@gal.step
Everything will be connected.
Not just people—but their stuff.
So the freezer tells the TV
if it is not full enough.
When everything is digital,
cars and toasters will converse.
That's supposed to make life easy.
What if it just makes life worse?

From robin@bea.b
When it's time to take vacations,
we can blast off to the stars
or hang out closer to the Earth
on Venus or on Mars.

From tessa@adrian.pat
Will this be the century of such immense technology
that words like "famine"—words like "war"—
will be old-fashioned words we won't need anymore?

1993 William Jefferson Clinton
becomes the forty-second
president of the United
States.

"Communications and
commerce are global . . .
technology is almost
magical."—Bill Clinton

". . . we have a bridge to
build to the 21st Century."
—Bill Clinton

91

At the Edge of the 21st Century

▧ Imagine!

CALEB GODDARD

Baton Rouge, Louisiana, December 31, 1999

Tomorrow a new century begins.
Tonight the sky throbs with so many stars.
So many stars, so many possibilities.
We might cast a line and reach . . . infinity.

Tonight the sky throbs with so many stars.
A hundred years ago, no one could know.
We might cast a line and reach . . . infinity.
Imagine! The Web is just a click away.

A hundred years ago, no one could know.
Kids like you and me—electronic spiderlings.
Imagine! The Web is just a click away.
Everyone on Earth can be connected.

Kids like you and me—electronic spiderlings.
So many stars, so many possibilities.
Everyone on Earth can be connected.
Tomorrow a new century begins.

A NOTE FROM THE AUTHOR

History comes alive for me when I can experience it through a specific person—someone whose face I can see and whose feelings I can imagine, someone with a name. The Holocaust with its millions of victims left me numb with horror. The intimate words of Anne Frank, a young Dutch girl living in hiding with her family in an attic, put the horror on a human scale. I could cry for Anne and begin to understand that for every number there was a person. Later I began to read the books of Studs Terkel. They're compilations of brief interviews with Americans, one person after another speaking out until their voices blend into a kind of American cantata. Perhaps these influences were what led me to assign a name, a place, and a date to all the poems in this collection. I hope the speakers in the poems will step off the pages to engage you in their lives.

Writing the poems became an ongoing process of listening for voices as I immersed myself in a wonderful hodgepodge of diaries, journals, biographies, and letters, as well as collections of photographs and paintings. Along the way I heard the voices of the famous—George Washington, Harriet Tubman, the Wright brothers—as well as people who were real but not enduringly famous, such as those teenage bandits Cattle Annie and Little Britches, or the skyscraper architect William Van Alen. I also heard the voices of fictional people who became very real to me. I wove them out of the threads of interviews I read or faces I saw. And finally I recycled my own memories, recalling just how it was to go shopping at the "five and ten," to do my bit for the war effort, or to climb on the bus for a ride to Washington in support of the civil rights bill.

Some of the things I learned made me think about history in a new way. For example, there is no evidence that human life developed gradually in either North or South America, as it did in Asia or Africa. About 35,000 years ago, probably driven to find game by the glaciers of the Ice Age, "The First Americans," the ancestors of modern Native Americans, began entering what is now Alaska from Asia. As they made their way down into the new world, they added the sounds of human voices to those of the birds and animals. That idea fills me with wonder, and I hope my poem will let you stretch your imagination back, back, back over the centuries to think about it.

In 1699 the population of the colonies was estimated at 262,000; one third were indentured servants. Some colonies, eager to boost population, offered an additional incentive of land to whoever sponsored a new settler. The masters paid the cost of a servant's passage in exchange for five years of unpaid labor. Sometimes these servants were treated worse than slaves and worked to death before their five years were up. It seems a bitter irony that when the captain of a Dutch ship traded his human cargo for food in Virginia in 1639, the Africans were given their freedom and full rights after five years. The idea of Africans as slaves came later.

How very hard life was in those tiny, unpainted houses of the seventeenth century! It still takes time to whip up a meal from supermarket fixings to cook on my gas stove, but what if I had to grow every bit of the food and then stand in a drafty fireplace to cook it? I'd never find time to write a poem or keep a daily journal, yet somehow, even in the seventeenth century, there were women who did.

Another new impression I hope to share is the effect of the seemingly boundless primary-growth forests, the gigantic trees—the dazzling green—on Europeans. The primary woodlands that once covered Europe and England were long gone. In the poem "To Hans in Germany," I helped Solomon Hess write a letter to Germany about the expansive new world.

Again and again my research made me treasure democracy, which is all too easy for us to take for granted. I never realized how much the early presidents struggled with the question of what their roles should be as leaders of a democracy. Exactly how did the constitution intend the executive branch of government to function? Was it ever proper to try to influence Congress? Should the president be formal and dignified, available to the public but only at a distance, or was he free to live as simply as he wished? Should he try to demonstrate democratic ideals in his very style of entertaining? Thomas Jefferson had a French cook and loved fine wines and small dinner parties with lively conversations; he installed round tables at the White House to make all seating positions equal. At his large dinners, as opposed to the small supper described in "My White House Education," the food was delivered to the dining room on dumbwaiters and guests served themselves to avoid any hint of favoritism. And through the nineteenth century a presidential candidate, once nominated, did not campaign on his own behalf. What would those political leaders think of politics today?

Sometimes surprising discoveries started with a picture. A brief caption under a photograph of an eagle identified as Old Abe, the Civil War mascot of the Wisconsin 8th, sent me searching for more information. Did Old Abe have anything to do with the eagle's becoming the symbol of the United States? Indeed he did. Before the company disbanded, the governor of Wisconsin gave Old Abe a home in the basement of the state capitol. The eagle started a new career as a fund-raiser, traveling to exhibitions and parades, where his pictures were sold. He even learned to sign them with a peck of his beak.

Little human details from letters and journals, which aren't found in more formal accounts, or sometimes even a dry document became kindling for a poem. Jamestown was the first settlement, which the British sponsored. It was a business undertaking. Unlike the Pilgrims, who set off more or less as families, only men and boys sailed for Jamestown. They were prepared to build. The passenger list of their ship, the *Godspeed*, made that clear. There were craftsmen such as carpenters and glaziers aboard, as well as laborers, gentlemen, and four boys. I knew nothing about Nathaniel Peacock except his name and the fact that he was a boy, but I got to know Captain John Smith, who became the leader of the settlement, better than I know most of my neighbors. Here was a man with a generosity of spirit, boundless enthusiasm, respect for the Indians, and even a sense of humor. Through him I learned about Wahunsonacock, the chief of the Powhatan villages. And through Smith's later letters I learned how the Pilgrims were sabotaged by their own suspicions as they prepared for their journey to the New World. The Pilgrim leaders spent about two weeks in Plymouth, England, making last-minute arrangements and bad bargains. Meanwhile, the *Mayflower*—packed with the crew, the Pilgrims, and their indentured servants— was anchored offshore. They all knew that repairs to a second ship, the *Speedwell*, had not made it seaworthy and that supplies were limited. What was it like to be a kid, waiting to sail? How much excitement did Pilgrim decorum allow? I decided to let "A Pilgrim Boy" speak for himself and learned that faith overcame fear.

I got to know William Bradford, the second governor of the Plymouth Colony, from excerpts of his history of the Pilgrims, *Of Plimoth Plantation*. We hear much of Squanto and the first Thanksgiving. Squanto had been kidnapped by an earlier visitor to New England, Captain Hunt, and sold as a slave in Spain. Squanto escaped to England. At last he got back to his village, only to find he was its sole survivor. A plague, probably cholera, had annihilated his loved ones, which Bradford self-righteously considered a blessing. Weren't the morally superior Pilgrims entitled to Squanto's services and the cleared fields of his village? Who were the villagers? Merely savages.

Perhaps the relationship between the settlers and the Native Americans would have been different had circumstances not caused, first, Captain Smith and, later, William Penn to return to England just when their leadership was so desperately needed in the colonies. There were many times that I said, "If only . . ." or "What if . . ." as I found voices for a poem. When my editor wanted a poem about the Trail of Tears, the forced removal of the Cherokee to Oklahoma when gold was discovered on their land in Georgia, I resisted—but weakly. I knew she was right, but I dreaded returning to such a sad story. When I did, I learned that the Cherokee had brought their case to the Supreme Court, which ruled in favor of the tribe. A brash frontiersman with a "clean 'em out" attitude, President Andrew Jackson wasn't about to let a bunch of judges stop him. What had happened to the system of checks and balances that the constitution had created? What if John Quincy Adams had won the election? If only . . .

At the beginning of the eighteenth century, could anyone have dreamed that the American colonies would become an independent nation? At the beginning of the nineteenth century, people and information could only travel as fast as horses could gallop or boats could sail. Thomas Jefferson had a vision of one country expanding to the Pacific Ocean. But how would one coast communicate with the other? While Jefferson pondered the possibilities of hot-air balloons, there's no evidence that he ever considered faster, power-driven ground transportation. Just imagine—two thousand British troops were killed at New Orleans in the most decisive American land victory of the War of 1812. A peace agreement had been signed more than two weeks earlier in Europe, but the news hadn't reached Washington.

Change, however, was coming. During the Civil War President Lincoln could confer with his generals by telegraph. And when the miles of telegraph lines reached San Francisco, the Pony Express was put out of business, only eighteen months after it was started. By 1869 the Union Pacific and the Central Pacific lines met in Utah to create a transcontinental railroad. At the Centennial Exhibition of 1876, Alexander Graham Bell was demonstrating his telephone. As the nineteenth century ended, a very few of the very rich even had what seemed to be nearly useless new toys— automobiles. Bicycles, however, were within the reach of almost any budget, thanks to competition. People and information were moving faster and faster.

As the twenty-first century begins, people, information, and materials whiz down highways and across skyways at speeds undreamed of a hundred years ago. Computers and the Internet are revolutionizing how we communicate, work, shop, explore, create, and learn. It is faster and easier to circle the globe than it was to cross the country fifty years ago. Where will the twenty-first century take us? Or perhaps a better question is, "Where shall we take the twenty-first century?" For it is people who can have ideas, create machines, build cities. We can treasure or trash our green land and the planet Earth. We can preserve and expand our precious democracy by being well-informed, thinking citizens, or we can lose it by goofing off. It's easy to let ourselves be jerked around by sound bites and the slick propaganda of special-interest groups. So listen up. Make sure you hear the voices of ALL the people. What is your voice saying? It's important. You're making history.

—*Bobbi Katz*

ACKNOWLEDGMENTS

Many thanks to the librarians and representatives of historical societies across the United States who helped me make these poems authentic. And to Studs Turkel, my hero.
—Bobbi Katz

BIBLIOGRAPHY
We the People
The American Indian, adapted for young readers by Anne Terry White, from text by William Brandon (New York: Random House, 1963).

Good Wives: Image and Reality in the Lives of Women in Northern New England, 1650–1750, by Laurel Thatcher Ulrich (New York: Knopf, 1982). Historian Laurel Thatcher Ulrich's scholarly books are packed with details of daily life.

At the Edge of the 18th Century
America at 1750: A Social Portrait, by Richard Hofstadter (New York: Random House, 1971).

American Scripture: Making the Declaration of Independence, by Pauline Maier (New York: Knopf, 1997).

Angel in the Whirlwind: The Triumph of the American Revolution, by Benson Bobrick (New York: Simon & Schuster, 1997).

The California Missions: A Pictorial History, by the Editorial Staff of Sunset Books (Menlo Park, CA: Lane, 1964).

Everyday Life in Early America, by David Freeman Hawke (New York: Harper & Row, 1988).

Washington, the Indispensable Man, by James Flexner (Boston: Little, Brown, 1994).

At the Edge of the 19th Century
Abraham Lincoln: The War Years, by Carl Sandburg (New York: Harcourt, Brace, 1939).

Edison: Inventing the Century, by Neil Baldwin (New York: Hyperion, 1995).

George Eastman and the Early Photographers, by Brian Coe (London: Priory Press, 1973).

A Midwife's Tale: The Life of Martha Ballard, Based on Her Diary, 1785–1812, by Laurel Thatcher Ulrich (New York: Vintage Books, 1991).

Old Abe the War Eagle: A True Story of the Civil War and Reconstruction, by Richard Zeitlin (Madison, WI: The State Historical Society of Wisconsin, 1986).

The Settlers' West, by Martin F. Schmitt and Dee Brown (New York: Ballantine, 1955).

Tenting Tonight: The Soldier's Life, by James Robertson, Jr., and the Editors of Time-Life Books (Alexandria, VA: Time-Life, 1984).

Trail of Tears: The Rise and Fall of the Cherokee Nation, by John Ehle (New York: Doubleday, 1988).

Undaunted Courage: Meriwether Lewis, Thomas Jefferson, and the Opening of the American West, by Stephen E. Ambrose (New York: Simon & Schuster, 1996).

With Malice Toward None: The Life of Abraham Lincoln, by Stephen B. Oates (New York: Harper & Row, 1977).

At the Edge of the 20th Century
1898: The Birth of the American Century, by David Traxel (New York: Knopf, 1998).

Children of the Dust Bowl: The True Story of the School at Weedpatch Camp, by Jerry Stanley (New York: Crown, 1992).
My tongue gets dry and my ears ache with the sound of wind when I even think of this book for young readers. It combines the story of migrants from the Oklahoma Panhandle during the 1930s with an inspiring account of what one determined teacher accomplished at a federal farm-labor camp in California.

Coming Apart; An Informal History of America in the 1960s, by William O'Neill (Chicago: Quadrangle Books, 1971).

Eleanor: The Years Alone, by Joseph P. Lash (New York: Norton, 1972).

"Life Was Meant to Be Lived": A Centenary Portrait of Eleanor Roosevelt, by Joseph P. Lash (New York: Norton, 1984).

Manzanar, by John C. Armor and Peter Wright, with photographs by Ansel Adams and commentary by John Hersey (New York: Times Books, 1988).
This book documents life at the first of ten camps where Japanese Americans were interned during World War II. Beautifully designed, it has an informative and moving text that complements the photographs.

Milestones of the Air: Jane's 100 Significant Aircraft, compiled by H. F. King and edited by John Taylor (New York: McGraw-Hill, 1969).

A Nation Divided: The Vietnam Experience, by Clark Dougan, Samuel Lipsman, and the Editors of Boston Publishing Company (Boston: Boston Publishing, 1984).

The Skyscraper, by Paul Goldberger (New York: Knopf, 1982).

The Smithsonian Book of Flight, by Walter J. Boyne (Washington, D.C.: Smithsonian Books, 1987).

Theodore Roosevelt's Letters to His Children, edited by Joseph Bucklin Bishop (New York: Scribner's, 1919).
The letters reveal a loving husband and a father who *really* plays with his kids. Honesty, courage, being a good sport—these are the values he gives them. We glimpse a more leisurely pace of life in the White House, even though the fearless president might lead visitors into the icy Potomac for a swim.

We Were Soldiers Once—and Young: Ia Drang, the Battle that Changed the War in Vietnam, by Lt. Gen. Harold G. Moore and Joseph L. Galloway (New York: Random House, 1992).

General

Alistair Cooke's America, by Alistair Cooke (New York: Knopf, 1980).

The Americans: The History of a People and a Nation, by Winthrop Jordan, M. Greenblatt, and J. S. Bowes (New York: McDougal, Littell, 1985).

American Ways of Life, by George R. Stewart (Garden City, NY: Doubleday, 1954).

Cowboy Culture: A Saga of Five Centuries, by David Dary (New York: Knopf, 1981).

A Nation of Nations: The People Who Came to America As Seen Through Objects and Documents Exhibited at the Smithsonian Institution, edited by Peter Marzio (New York: Harper & Row, 1976).
This is a book I've been feasting on for many years. With 670 pages, it's a veritable banquet of Americana: objects, information, photos, and engravings from the nation's earliest beginnings to the 1960s.

The President's House, by William Seale (Washington, D.C.: The White House Historical Association, 1986).

Promise and Betrayal: Voices from the Struggle for Women's Emancipation (1776–1920): A Dramatic Reading, by Carol Hanisch (Port Ewen, NY: Truth-Tellers, 1997).
Uses the riveting words of people speaking out for freedom and equality for African Americans and for women. It covers the period between 1796 and 1920, when the 19th Amendment was passed. At a dramatic reading I attended, seven readers each took several parts; an eighth sang songs. Later I wrote "A Song for Suffrage."

We Lived There, Too: In Their Own Words—Pioneer Jews and the Westward Movement of America, 1630–1930, by Kenneth Libo and Irving Howe (New York: St. Martin's, 1984).

A NOTE ABOUT THE ARTWORK

The front cover:

1	2	3	4		5
6	7	8		9	10
11	12	13	14	15	16
	17	18			19
17	20	21	22	23	
24	25			26	27
28	29	30	31		32

1. Black Hawk (Ma-ka-tae-mish-kia-kiak), 1767–1838. Sac (Sauk) Indian chief. *Dictionary of American Portraits*, edited by Hayward and Blanche Cirker and the Staff of Dover Publications, Inc. (New York: Dover, 1967).

2. The Rev. Dr. Martin Luther King, Jr., 1929–1968, at a Miami news conference, August 16, 1965. Associated Press.

3. Mark Twain (Samuel Langhorne Clemens), 1835–1910. Novelist, humorist, lecturer. *Dictionary of American Portraits* (New York: Dover, 1967).

4. George Washington, 1732–1799, after a Gilbert Stuart portrait. *The American Revolution: A Picture Sketchbook*, by John Grafton (New York: Dover, 1975).

5. Evelyn Byrd, 1716–1737. Colonial belle, "Ghost of Westover." Courtesy Colonial Williamsburg. *Dictionary of American Portraits* (New York: Dover, 1967).

6. Renze A. McDowell in the 1950s. Photograph courtesy Virginia Duncan.

7. Abraham Lincoln, 1809–1865. Photograph by Alexander Hesler. *Dictionary of American Portraits* (New York: Dover, 1967).

8. Eagle. *The American Revolution: A Picture Sketchbook* (New York: Dover, 1975).

9. Crowd at John F. Kennedy rally, Upper Darby, PA, October 1960. Photographer Burton Berinsky, courtesy Helene Berinsky. Also used #26.

10. Emilio Aquinaldo, 1869–1964. Filipino patriot and insurrectionist. *Dictionary of American Portraits* (New York: Dover, 1967).

11. Thomas ("Tad") Lincoln, 1853–1871. Youngest son of Abraham Lincoln. Courtesy National Archives, Brady Collection. *Dictionary of American Portraits* (New York: Dover, 1967).

12. Ivy Johnson. Photographer Nina Crews, 1999.

13. Edith Wharton, 1862–1937. Novelist. Courtesy American Academy of Arts and Letters. *Dictionary of American Portraits* (New York: Dover, 1967).

14. Theodore Roosevelt, 1858–1919. *Dictionary of American Portraits* (New York: Dover, 1967).

15. Migrant agricultural worker, near Holtville, California. Photographer Dorothea Lange, 1937. Collection Farm Security Administration—Office of War Information Photograph Collection, Library of Congress.

16. Marian Anderson at memorial service for President John F. Kennedy, New York, NY, December 2, 1963. Photographer Burton Berinsky, courtesy Helene Berinsky.

17. Benjamin Franklin, 1706–1790. Printer, statesman, philosopher, inventor. In 1887 this page appeared in *Leslie's Magazine* commemorating the centennial of the Constitutional Convention. *The American Revolution: A Picture Sketchbook* (New York: Dover, 1975).

18. Neil Armstrong, 1930– . Apollo 11 Commander Neil Armstrong during suiting for the launch with astronauts Michael Collins and Edwin E. Aldrin, Jr., 1969. Collection NASA, Kennedy Space Center.

19. American Horse, *fl.* 1875–1905. Sioux chief. Courtesy Bureau of American Ethnology, Smithsonian Institution. *Dictionary of American Portraits* (New York: Dover, 1967).

20. Harriet Tubman, *c.* 1821–1913. Escaped slave, abolitionist. Courtesy Library of Congress. *Dictionary of American Portraits* (New York: Dover, 1967).

21. César Chávez, 1927–1993. Founder of the United Farm Workers. Photograph 1966. New York World-Telegram & Sun Collection, Library of Congress.

22. Japanese mother and daughter. Photographer Dorothea Lange, 1937. Collection Farm Security Administration—Office of War Information Photograph Collection, Library of Congress.

23. Jesse James, 1847–1882. Western outlaw. Courtesy Mercaldo Archives. *Dictionary of American Portraits* (New York: Dover, 1967).

24. Thomas Alva Edison, 1847–1931. Inventor. *Dictionary of American Portraits* (New York: Dover, 1967).

25. Lucy Stone, 1818–1893. Reformer, advocate of women's rights. Courtesy Tamiment Institute Library. *Dictionary of American Portraits* (New York: Dover, 1967).

26. See #9.

27. Beatrice and Sadie Rosenheim in the 1890s. Photograph courtesy Susan Hirschman.

28. Thomas Paine, 1737–1809. Revolutionary agitator, pamphleteer, philosopher; author of *The Age of Reason* and *Common Sense*. Engraved by Illman & Sons after a painting by George Romney. *Dictionary of American Portraits* (New York: Dover, 1967).

29. Christopher Columbus, *c.* 1446–1506. Explorer. Courtesy Eric Schaal. *Dictionary of American Portraits* (New York: Dover, 1967).

30. Buffalo Bill (William Frederick Cody), 1846–1917. Western scout, showman. Courtesy New-York Historical Society. *Dictionary of American Portraits* (New York, Dover: 1967).

31. Henry Ford, 1863–1947. Automobile manufacturer. Courtesy Automobile Manufacturers Association, Inc. *Dictionary of American Portraits* (New York: Dover, 1967).

32. Edward Winslow, 1595–1655. Mayflower Pilgrim; a founder and governor of Plymouth Colony. *Dictionary of American Portraits* (New York: Dover, 1967).

The interior images:

Title Page: Etchings of a Colonial-era ship, the stowage of a slave ship, and a butterfly were combined with a found photograph from the late 1800s, a silhouette copy of a lithograph of the first American railway train, a photograph of an airplane wing, and some potting soil.

The First Americans: A photograph of native plants of the Northeast and a photograph of a small stream were digitally combined with a tinted detail from "Shoshone Indian" (Thomas Nast Collection, copyright © Collection of the New-York Historical Society).

At the Edge of the 18th Century: Leaves, twigs, and acorns were combined with photographs of Northeastern woods; a tinted, altered detail from "William Penn Treaty with the Indians" (engraving copyright © Collection of the New-York Historical Society); and a map of Carolina published in 1682 (from the Library of Congress Geography and Map Division), re-photographed, and digitally enhanced.

At the Edge of the 19th Century: A model of a clapboard wall, stars, an etching of a Federal-era eagle, and etchings of musical instruments were combined with a tinted detail from "Unidentified Lady," by Moses B. Russell (1831, watercolor on paper, copyright © Collection of the New-York Historical Society), photographed, and digitally enhanced.

At the Edge of the 20th Century: Found photographs dating from the turn of the century were combined with an old watch face, and in the background a detail from "Broadway and 23rd Street, view from southeast with Fifth Avenue Hotel, Dewey Arch and cable car" (1899, unidentified photographer, copyright © Collection of the New-York Historical Society), re-photographed, and digitally enhanced.

At the Edge of the 21st Century: Photographs of four children (left to right: Shelby Garner, Alexandria Frank, Jonathan Sanchez, Jessica Cole), an aerial view somewhere in Michigan, and a starlit night sky were combined and re-photographed. Additional enhancements, including typography, were added digitally.